Date Due

POVERTY

Changing Attitudes 1900–2000

Teresa Garlake

RSVP

RAINTREE
STECK-VAUGHN
P U B L I S H E R S
A Steck-Vaughn Company

Austin, Texas

TWENTIETH CENTURY ISSUES SERIES

Censorship
Crime and Punishment
Medical Ethics
Poverty
Racism
Women's Rights

Published by Raintree Steck-Vaughn Publishers, an imprint of Steck-Vaughn Company

Library of Congress Cataloging-in-Publication Data
Garlake, Teresa.
Poverty / Teresa Garlake.
      p.   cm.—(20th Century Issues)
      Includes bibliographical references and index.
      ISBN 0-8172-5894-9
      1. Poverty—Juvenile literature.
      2. Poor—Public opinion—Juvenile literature.
      3. Charities—Juvenile literature.
      4. Economic assistance, Domestic—Juvenile literature.
      I. Title.
      HC79.P6G37   1999
      362.5'09'049—dc21   99-12578

Printed in Italy. Bound in the United States.
1 2 3 4 5 6 7 8 9 0 04 03 02 01 00

The author would like to dedicate this book to Esme and all her generation.

Picture acknowledgments
Associated Press/Topham 35; Corbis-Bettmann 16 (Riis), 17, 24, 28, 30-31, 36-37; Corbis-Bettmann/UPI 53; Mary Evans Picture Library 6, 11, 12, 13, 15, 20, 23; Hulton Getty Picture Collection 10, 19, 22, 25 (Kurt Hutton), 27, 34, 39 (Monty Fresco, Jr.), 44; National Museums and Galleries on Merseyside 33; Panos Pictures 4 (Philip Wolmuth), 7 (Jean-Leo Dugast), 8 (John Spaull), 14 (Sean Sprague), 21 (Penny Tweedie), 42 (Betty Press), 45 (Sean Sprague), 46 (Eric Miller), 48 (Rhodri Jones), 50 (Liba Taylor), 54 (Zed Nelson), 55 (Philip Wolmuth), 56 (Jim Holmes), 58 (Paul Smith); Popperfoto 32, 38; Topham Picturepoint 29; UNEP/Barbel Kreisl/Topham 5; UNEP/Iftekhar Ahmed/Topham 43; UNEP/Shadley Lombard/Topham 18; UPI/Corbis 40; Wayland Picture Library 47 (Howard J. Davies), 49 (Jimmy Holmes), 51 (Howard J. Davies), 52 (Howard J. Davies), 57, 59.

Cover: main picture shows women and children searching a dump for materials to recycle (UNEP/Iftekhar Ahmed/Topham); black-and-white pictures show, top to bottom, a communal soup kitchen in Hammersmith, London, May 1917; a homeless man on the streets in the 1970s (Mary Evans Picture Library); and children "holding onto life" in 1995 (UNEP/T Stoddart/Topham).

CONTENTS

What is poverty? 4

A history of poverty 8

Divided societies 14

The Great Depression 22

Winds of change 30

Responses to poverty... 38

The changing face of aid... 46

Looking to the future 55

Glossary 60

Books to read... 61

Useful addresses... 62

Index.. 63

WHAT IS POVERTY?

At the end of the twentieth century, more than a billion people in the world live in poverty. We all have a picture in our minds of what it means to be poor—from images of malnourished people on television to a person begging in the streets. But what is meant by the word "poverty?"

Poverty has many different faces. It can mean not having an education and thus missing the chance for a better job. You might think that at the end of the

In the rich world, the poor are often still forced to beg for a living.

Poverty on the sidewalk—South American street children

twentieth century no one should be deprived of the chance to learn. Yet our world remains a divided place. Over 140 million of the world's children between the ages of six and eleven do not go to school. Poverty may mean being forced to live in a refugee camp. One person out of every 120 has had to leave home because of war.

Sometimes poverty is obvious. In the early years of the twentieth century, Jack London, an American novelist and journalist, described how he could find the misery of poverty only five minutes' walk from any point in London. But poverty is also hidden. The person trying to live on Social Security who must choose between staying warm in the winter or having enough to eat does so in private. In poorer parts of the world, far from the paved roads that sweep from city to city, a farmer whose crops have failed goes hungry and unnoticed.

OPINION

"Poverty is hunger, loneliness, nowhere to go when the day is over, deprivation, discrimination, abuse, and illiteracy."
Single mother from Guyana

OPINION

"I've been living in a tent for six months. It's hard at first to fall asleep. It's cold, but you get used to it."
Sixteen-year-old homeless man

5

This Victorian cartoon gives two views of poverty. The images inside the eyeglasses show how rich people believe the poor live. The other images show the stark reality.

Poverty has never been easy to define—in the Persian language there are thirty different words to name those who are poor. The Elizabethans in England saw the poor as two different groups. The old or the sick were seen to be "deserving," because they were unable to work and support themselves. The "undeserving" poor were those who, in theory, had brought their troubles upon themselves. They were seen as lazy, and possibly criminal. Other societies have viewed poverty in very different ways. In many Eastern traditions, people who choose to share the life of the poor are respected and admired. The prophet Mohammed is believed to have said "poverty is my pride and glory." All Muslims are required to give a certain amount of what they have to the poor. Those who receive such charity are not expected to feel shame or obligation.

ABSOLUTE OR RELATIVE?

At the beginning of the century, researchers tended to use a definition of absolute poverty. They looked at a person's basic biological needs for food, water, shelter, and clothing. If these needs were not met, they were considered poor. This definition continues to exist. In the recent past, politicians have used a definition of absolute poverty to argue that poverty does not exist in the developed world—after all, they argue, large numbers of people are not starving.

However, more people now agree that poverty is also relative. The definition of relative poverty is reached by comparing the standard of living of one person with that of another person in the same community. In 1990, at least two out of every three people in Great Britain thought that housing with an indoor toilet and bath, heating, carpeting, a refrigerator, washing machine, three meals a day, and toys for their children were basic necessities. At the turn of the century, some of these items did not even exist. Comparisons are difficult to make across time and culture, and the definition of relative poverty is not fixed.

The United Nations Development Program (UNDP) uses a human poverty index to measure poverty in different countries. This index is based on the belief that a person's sense of well-being and happiness is as important as their wealth. Even the poorest people lead valuable and valued lives. The human poverty index brings together a variety of different elements—length of life, access to education, and standard of living—to measure poverty.

Whatever shape it takes, poverty casts a long shadow. It is about more than just money. In whatever age they live, the poor do not have the same opportunities as others. They lose something very precious: the chance for a long, healthy, creative, and happy life.

In the Buddhist tradition, poverty is revered. These monks are receiving alms (gifts of charity) from a follower.

A HISTORY OF POVERTY

So far, we have looked at how poverty affects individuals. Poverty also burdens countries. If you look at the map (opposite), you will see that our world is divided into rich and poor countries. Many of the world's poorer countries were once colonies. Most northern countries are richer than the southern countries. Not all southern countries are poor, of course—Saudi Arabia, for instance, has generated great wealth by oil exports. Nor are all northern countries rich. In eastern Europe and the former Soviet Union, poverty has recently become a major problem. Between 1988 and 1994, the number of poor people in the region increased from fourteen million to more than 119 million.

In Armenia and many other countries in eastern Europe, the collapse of the Soviet Union led to great social hardship.

The rich-poor divide between countries has not always existed. When Europeans first reached the Americas and Africa they were impressed with what they found. A Dutch merchant who visited the West African empire of Benin just before 1600 was struck by its size and splendor; another praised its "good laws" and "well-organized police." In Latin America, before 1500, the Incas built over 8,700 mi. (14,000 km) of paved roads, with bridges and tunnels crossing mountainous terrain. Early European travelers encountered very diverse societies. Many, such as the Aztecs in Latin America and the Moguls in India, were highly divided between rich and poor. Other subsistence societies, such as the !Kung of the Kalahari or the Maori of New Zealand, were much more equal. In these latter societies, communities were based on a strong network of kinship ties.

THE SLAVE TRADE

The divisions between countries began when Christopher Columbus landed in the Caribbean in 1492. The Spanish conquerors wanted to take back to Europe as much silver and gold as they could. They set the indigenous people to work in mines and established plantations where crops such as sugar and tobacco were grown. But the diseases the Europeans brought with them, such as smallpox, measles, and influenza, combined with war and overwork to wipe out millions of American Indians. More labor was needed, so the Europeans turned their eyes toward Africa.

> **OPINION**
>
> "What thoughtful rich people call the problem of poverty, thoughtful poor people call with equal justice a problem of riches."
> R. H. Tawney, historian, 1913

The map shows the invisible line that divides our world into rich and poor. This definition of the rich-poor divide was first developed by the Brandt Commission in 1980. (See page 51.)

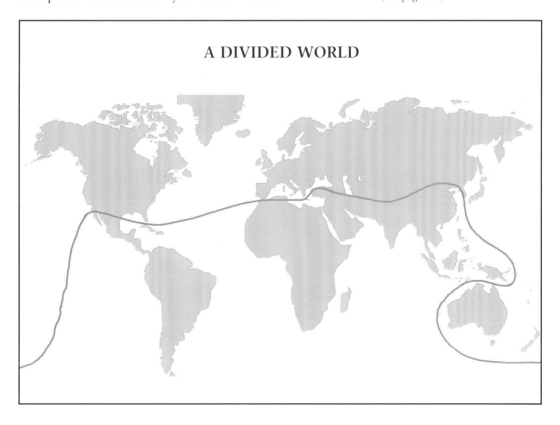

A DIVIDED WORLD

An African slave market in 1870. All of those taken as slaves were young and healthy.

The slave trade helped to lay the foundations for our unequal world. European countries sold cloth and guns to African slave traders. Slaves were captured and taken to work unpaid on plantations in the Americas, and the crops they grew were sold in Europe for large profits. The slave trade was the largest forced migration in history and did untold damage to Africa's development. By the time slavery was abolished in the nineteenth century, between ten and twelve million Africans had been sold in the Americas. A further two million died before they landed, as a result of the appalling conditions on board the slave ships.

Wealth from the slave trade helped Europe's industrial revolution take place. It paid for new factories and machines. From the late eighteenth century onward, machines were made that could produce more goods at greater speed. This meant greater profits for the factory owners. Modern poverty is often traced back to this time. As large numbers of people were drawn from the countryside to work in factories, cities grew. People who had left the land could no longer grow their own food. They needed their wages to survive. If they became sick and could not work, or if their wages fell, they became poor.

At this time, some rich individuals used their personal wealth to relieve poverty. These "philanthropists" were often motivated by religious beliefs. In Great Britain, Cadbury, the Quaker family of chocolate manufacturers, moved their chocolate factory from central Birmingham to the village of Bournville, on the outskirts of the city. The factory workers and their families were able to leave the unhealthy slums of the inner city for a cleaner environment with green open spaces. Other industrialists who used their wealth to improve the lives of poorer people were Seebohm Rowntree and Joseph Fry and, in the United States, Andrew Carnegie and John D. Rockefeller.

Working in a cloth factory at the turn of the century. The photo is carefully posed—conditions were generally much worse than this.

THE COLONIES

European manufacturers needed market places to sell their goods, and raw materials to keep their industries going. Toward the end of the nineteenth century, European powers started to take over countries in Africa and Asia. The European armies used sophisticated new weapons to crush any resistance. By 1914, Europe and North America controlled eighty-four percent of the world's land.

The colonies became a way of transferring wealth back to Europe. The colonizers wanted to exploit the resources of the colonies in the most efficient way possible. Land that had been used for growing food for the local people was taken to create large estates. There the colonizers grew cash crops for export. Farmers in Portuguese Mozambique, for instance, were forced to grow cotton and sell it very cheaply. They then paid much higher prices for imported cotton clothes, which had been manufactured in Portugal. Cotton came to be known as "the mother of poverty" and, a few decades later, cotton-growing areas became famine stricken.

South Africa's diamond mines brought wealth to European companies, but not to local people. Black workers were physically exhausted and cruelly treated.

Gradually the colonies were divided into different zones. Mines and plantations were developed in profitable zones, closely linked to the sea by rail and road. The men who worked there had been squeezed out of the rural areas by the need to earn money. These migrant laborers were paid the wages of single men, but still supported their families, whom they had been forced to leave, destitute, in rural areas. Thus was the worst poverty hidden from the view of the outside world.

With the colonizers came missionaries, who often helped break down traditional African authority.

Many Europeans saw themselves as members of a superior race, bringing "the inestimable benefits of civilization" to "downtrodden" peoples. They believed that colonialism would help "backward" societies to develop. Help for the poor was provided by missionaries who set up basic education and health services. Missionaries extolled the virtues of hard work and respect for authority, and thus helped to gain acceptance of colonial rule. However, they also sowed seeds of discontent, as they preached that all people were equal before God.

So it was against this backdrop of global inequality that the twentieth century dawned. And although these events happened long ago, their effects are still felt today. However, while colonialism helped to create a world divided into rich and poor, there were other factors at play too. In the next chapter we look at divisions within societies and see how these have often contributed to the burden of poverty.

KEY MOMENT

The Scramble for Africa

At the Berlin Conference in 1884–1885, the countries of Europe agreed to divide up what King Leopold of Belgium called "this magnificent African cake." Europeans used military force to take over the largely unexplored continent of Africa. Their occupation allowed Europe to grow rich, but most Africans feel that they lost far more than they gained. Much of Africa's poverty today is a legacy of colonialism.

DIVIDED SOCIETIES

Today the lifestyle of the Maasai in Kenya is still based on cooperation and self-sufficiency.

Societies have always been divided: even the earliest social groups were made up of people who served different functions within their communities. But societies have not always been divided along the lines of wealth, with some people rich and others poor. Many ancient societies were subsistence communities where people lived by hunting and gathering food or by growing just enough to support themselves. These communities had developed intricate ways of living in balance with nature. No single person or group had control over the resources (such as land and water) on which others depended. The survival of the whole community depended on cooperation, and no one person was much richer than anyone else.

With the development of agriculture, civilizations became more complex. Groups that did not work on the land began to be supported by others that did. Gradually, societies became more unequal. As long ago as 250 B.C., the Romans employed huge numbers of slaves. Much later, in A.D. 1438, the Incas began to establish a huge empire in Latin America. This empire was immensely powerful and it was based on inequality. At the top was a god king, who was given tribute by thousands of peasants.

CLASS DISTINCTIONS

Social divisions in the twentieth century, as in any other, have often made poverty worse. In Great Britain and other parts of Europe, social divisions have traditionally been along class lines. In the nineteenth century, the upper classes dominated the country. They gained their wealth from the land they owned. As a privileged group, they seldom worked and they enjoyed the education of the best private schools followed by university. With the industrial revolution, many factory owners were able to join the upper classes by virtue of the wealth they had accumulated. But the vast armies of people who went to work in cities owned no land and could live only by working for low wages.

OPINION

In 1943, the author George Orwell made the following observations about the British class system: "...newcomers to England are still astonished and sometimes horrified by the blatant differences between class and class. The majority of the people can still be 'placed' in an instant by their manners, clothes, and general appearance... but the most striking difference of all is in language and accent... And though class distinctions do not exactly coincide with economic distinctions, the contrast between wealth and poverty is very much more taken for granted than in most countries."

Members of the British upper class enjoy a river trip on Ascot Sunday in 1914.

New York City, 1910: early in the century it was not uncommon for a working-class family to live in just one room.

By the early years of the twentieth century, most people belonged to the working class and were defined by the type of work they did, or their lack of work. Working-class children were much more likely to live in poverty. They usually lived in poor-quality, damp housing without running water, where illnesses such as tuberculosis could easily spread. They rarely stayed in school beyond the minimum age.

As the commercial and administrative sectors expanded, so did the middle class. This was made up of non-manual workers who often had professions. The middle class was sometimes called the "servant-keeping class."

There have never been clear boundaries between the classes, but they have always led very different lives, with wealth distributed unevenly between them. In 1936 and 1938, one percent of Great Britain's richest people owned fifty-five percent of the country's wealth. Three-quarters of the population could have sold all they owned for less than £100 (approximately $3,500 today).

At the end of the twentieth century, many people argue that educational opportunities and improved living standards mean that the class system no longer exists. But the ways in which people move up or down in society have remained more or less the same. In Great Britain, you are five times more likely to stay in the top earning group of society if you are born into it. And you are just as likely to remain in the working class if born into this group.

THE AMERICAN DREAM

By 1900, the United States was the most industrialized nation in the world. The poor of Europe were attracted to it as a land of opportunity and freedom where anyone could become wealthy. In 1910, out of a population of ninety-two million Americans, well over thirteen million were foreign-born. Many had come to the United States in pursuit of "the American dream"—the belief that as prosperity grew everyone would be able to share its benefits.

But industrialization created huge gaps between rich and poor. While most people simply tried to earn enough to survive, the country boasted more than 4,000 millionaires at the turn of the century. In the years leading up to World War I, industrial tycoons competed to draw attention to their wealth. When he heard that another multimillionaire had left $80,000,000 at his death, oil industry magnate John D. Rockefeller is said to have remarked: "And we all thought he was rich!"

KEY MOMENT

World War I
World War I, which lasted from August 1914 to November 1918, was the first war to involve all the major powers. It resulted in a massive number of casualties, and major economies were ruined. Under the peace agreement, the Treaty of Versailles, Germany was required to pay reparations (costs) for the damage caused by the war. This created widespread poverty for the German people, which led to the rise of the National Socialists under Adolf Hitler.

Two young Polish women arrive in the U.S. in 1910 to make a new life.

THE CASTE SYSTEM

We have already seen how colonialism helped set up divisions within societies that made poverty worse. In many countries, colonial powers passed laws over the ownership of land. These often helped to ensure that the gulf between rich and poor continued, as it does in many cases to this day. However, inequalities and division also existed in many pre-colonial societies.

The caste system in India is probably the oldest hierarchical system in the world, with a history going back several thousand years. Although a hierarchical society does not necessarily bring about poverty for its people, in practice those from the lower castes tend to be poorer than those from the higher castes. The caste system is based upon the Hindu belief in reincarnation that states that the way in which people fulfill their place in this life will determine their position in the next. Every Hindu is born into a caste and cannot move out of it. Each caste is defined by a job. Those jobs which are seen as "polluting," such as sweeping, are done by lower castes. Outside the caste system are the "untouchables," who do the most poorly paid and "dirty" work.

A housing settlement in South Africa where wealth is still divided very unequally between white and black people

Religious and political movements have often challenged the caste system. From 1920 onward, Mohandas (Mahatma) Gandhi awakened India to the scandal of untouchability. He sought to improve the lot of "untouchables," who he renamed "harijans," meaning "people of God." While Gandhi worked to reform the caste system, other leaders sought to overthrow it. In 1956, Dr. B. R. Ambedkar, a harijan himself, converted to Buddhism together with four million of his followers in order to express discontent at the inequalities they faced.

In India today, discrimination by caste is outlawed. Harijans and other groups are now guaranteed a certain number of seats in parliament and a percentage of government jobs and educational opportunities. But despite these moves toward equality, harijans are still among the most disadvantaged groups in Indian society.

Mahatma Gandhi surrounded by supporters during a tour on behalf of "harijans"

OPINION

"And why do I regard British rule in India as a curse? It has impoverished the dumb millions by a system of progressive exploitation and by a ruinously expensive military and civil administration which they can never afford."
Mohandas Gandhi in a letter to Lord Irwin, 1930

POVERTY AND REVOLUTION

There has always been resistance to social inequalities, and this has brought about massive change. In the early years of the twentieth century, Russia was a country riddled by inequality. Nearly ninety percent of the people were peasants who lived in terrible poverty. As the growing population found it impossible to scratch a living from the land, there were massive migrations to the cities.

Lenin addresses workers and soldiers in 1917 at the start of the world's first workers' revolution.

Russia suffered heavily during World War I. Hundreds of thousands of peasants and workers lost their lives. War brought food shortages and rising prices. In March

1917, a demonstration of women joined 20,000 steel-workers on strike. Soon 90,000 workers were marching to the center of Petrograd. The next day, when bakeries ran out of bread, riots broke out.

The Russian ruler, the Czar, was forced to abdicate and a few months later the revolutionary Communists, under Vladimir Ilyich Lenin, seized power. They aimed to create a new, more equal society. Land was given to peasants, and workers took control of factories. The Russian Revolution was to reverberate around the world and shape twentieth century history. Between thirty and forty years later, one third of humanity found itself living in states that followed the Communist model.

However, as we look back over the twentieth century, we can see that the huge changes have not ended social divisions. Today, some groups are much more likely to live in poverty than others. Seventy percent of the world's poor are women. They work longer hours and are paid less than men for doing the same jobs. Girls tend to be taken out of school earlier than boys. Of the 900 million adults in the world who cannot read, two-thirds are women.

Aborigines are among the poorest groups in Australia. In the protest below, they are claiming the right to ancestral land that has been taken by mining companies.

Indigenous peoples are also more likely to experience poverty. In the United States, forty percent of indigenous Americans live below the poverty line. The disabled, the young, and the old all face disadvantage in our societies. The fruits of progress, it seems, are not shared by all.

THE GREAT DEPRESSION

World War I left Europe devastated. At first, the war seemed to bring prosperity. Millions of workers found jobs in factories, taking the places of men who had been called to fight. Women were recruited to the workforce in greater numbers than ever before. But as peace returned and wartime production ended, those who had fought in the muddy battlefields or worked in factories were expected to forget the promises of a better world. It seemed that a swift return to poverty was inevitable. The 1920s and 1930s were to see an economic decline that would threaten the stability of the industrialized world. To understand how this could happen we need to look to the United States.

A soldier who fought in World War I tries to earn a living as a street performer.

Investors flock to hear the latest news of share prices during the Wall Street Crash.

THE AMERICAN STOCK MARKET

The war had reinforced the United States' position as the largest industrial power in the world. It was also the world's biggest lender—in 1919, Great Britain owed the United States millions that it had borrowed to pay war debts. Many believed that America's economic progress was unstoppable. For the first time, ordinary people bought shares in the stock market, hoping to get rich quick. Nine million investors "speculated" by borrowing money to buy shares and hoping to resell them at a profit before they had to repay their debts.

A loser on the stock market tries to sell his car to avoid destitution.

OPINION

"We got more wheat, more corn, more food, more money in the banks, more everything in the world than any nation that ever lived ever had, yet we are starving to death. We are the first nation in the history of the world to go to the poor-house in an automobile."
Will Rogers, American humorist, 1931

However, by 1927 there were signs that this boom could not last. American agriculture was in decline, with more and more farmers declaring bankruptcy. More consumer goods were produced than the population was able to buy. Sales of automobiles declined and fewer houses were being built. High foreign tariffs meant that international trade was decreasing. The bubble of prosperity burst when share prices on the New York Stock Exchange on Wall Street collapsed and thousands of Americans were reduced to poverty almost overnight.

With the Wall Street Crash, American loans to other countries were called in, and the Great Depression began. The end of U.S. loans meant that Europe was pushed into an economic crisis and millions faced unemployment and poverty. In Great Britain in 1932, almost a quarter of those who wanted work could not find it. Unemployment was at its worst in heavily industrialized areas such as South Wales and northeast England. When Palmers' shipyard closed in 1933, eight out of every ten workers were left without jobs. Charities set up soup kitchens to feed the hungry. Workers organized "Hunger Marches" and advanced on London to denounce the politicians they believed were responsible for their poverty.

KEY MOMENT

The Wall Street Crash
In the late 1920s, the American stock market on Wall Street, New York, began to look less secure. On October 29, 1929—Black Tuesday—investors rushed to sell their shares while prices were still high. But with everyone selling and no one buying, prices plummeted. Sixteen million shares were sold at a loss of $10 billion. This was the worst day in the history of the New York stock market. Thousands of investors were ruined overnight and plunged into poverty.

An unemployed man in Wigan, England in 1939

THE GERMAN DEBT

Germany was also hit hard by the Great Depression. In 1921, Germany was presented with a war reparations bill that would amount to well over $1 trillion today. With an economy in ruins after the excesses of war, there was no way that the German nation could meet such massive debts. The government began printing large amounts of money, but this caused massive price rises. Money became worthless. In 1923, a year of hyperinflation, millions of people faced starvation.

The German people suffered enormously. The Department of Health was alarmed at the steep rise in infant mortality. It also reported that as many as one in five children had to be turned away from school because they were not strong enough. A school inspector from Leipzig found that out of a class of twenty-seven girls, only three had adequate clothing and only four had enough to eat. The German people felt angry at what they believed was an unjust peace. Their view was supported by influential thinkers around the world.

By 1932, forty-four percent of Germans were unemployed. In this climate of poverty and insecurity, it was easy for extremism to take hold. The National Socialist (Nazi) party promised an end to Germany's humiliation. In the 1930 elections, the Nazis became the second-largest group in parliament. In 1933, the National Socialist leader, Adolf Hitler, became Chancellor and set about bringing the economy under control. Between 1933 and 1938, Germany was the most successful state at reducing poverty.

Elsewhere in central and eastern Europe, countries struggled to pay off their debts by selling wheat. But since prices were so low there, people endured terrible hardship. Like many of the German people, they searched for someone to blame. More and more countries became hostile toward the minorities who lived among them, and Jews found themselves increasingly discriminated against.

ECONOMIC COLLAPSE

The effects of the Wall Street Crash reverberated far beyond Europe. Between 1929 and 1932, international trade slumped by sixty percent. This hit colonies particularly hard because they depended on the export of certain raw materials. Farmers tried to compensate for falling prices by growing and selling more crops. But oversupply just meant that prices

In 1923, German money had become so worthless that children used piles of banknotes as toys.

plunged further still. In Brazil, cash crops became so worthless that coffee-growers used coffee instead of coal to fuel their railroad steam engines. In the West Indies, producers depended entirely on British and American markets. As those markets collapsed, wages were cut. Many plantations were closed down and unemployment rose sharply resulting, eventually, in riots, strikes, and a campaign to end British rule.

The hungry share some bread during the Russian famine of 1921.

Richer peasants, like these in 1930 who did not support collectivization, were forced to leave their villages.

Only one major country was unaffected by the Great Depression. After the Russian Revolution, the Soviet Union was cut off from the rest of Europe and began to develop its own industries. However, the revolutionaries were faced not only with hostility from the outside world, but also with a civil war. By 1921, agricultural production had collapsed. Drought caused a massive famine that killed over five million peasants. The crisis prompted Lenin to relax controls and allow private trade again. However, after Lenin's death, Stalin began to force individual farmers to work on large, collective farms. Food was taken to feed workers in the cities. However, in the countryside it was a different story. There was a decrease in the amount of food produced. Collectivization left a legacy of hatred in the countryside.

The Great Depression shook the foundations of societies in the twentieth century. The security and standards of living that many people took for granted were not as solid as they had once thought. The poverty of the 1920s and 1930s led to fears of revolution and instability. It contributed to the causes of World War II. But it also led to calls for an end to unemployment and a general feeling that more should be done by the state to alleviate poverty.

KEY MOMENT

Collectivization in the Soviet Union

After the Russian Revolution, the state needed a reliable source of food to feed the growing number of workers in the factories. From 1929 on, Soviet peasants were forced to pool their land and equipment and work collectively. For the poorer peasants who had hoped that the revolution would give them their own plots of land, this was a huge disappointment. Peasants fiercely resisted collectivization by reducing what they grew and by slaughtering their animals. Thousands who resisted were sent to forced labor camps in Siberia. Within ten years, ninety-eight percent of Russian farmland had been collectivized.

WINDS OF CHANGE

Many people had feared that the poverty of the Great Depression would overwhelm the stability of the industrial nations. There was a growing feeling that the state should do more to relieve hardship. When Franklin D. Roosevelt became president of the United States in 1933, he accepted that the problems of poverty and unemployment could not be dealt with by private charities or individuals alone. He launched the "New Deal." As part of this, Roosevelt's government set up a number of organizations designed to bring hope to poverty-stricken Americans. One of the most successful was the Works Progress Administration (WPA). it created work projects for which workers were paid about $52 a month. The pay was barely enough for a family to live on, but for many it was a lifeline. In eight years, the WPA employed 8.5 million people and spent $11 billion. By 1941, it had built or improved over 2,500 hospitals, 5,900 school buildings, and nearly 13,000 playgrounds.

STATE INTERVENTION

Under the New Deal, the state became involved in creating jobs on a large scale. This had never been done before. Also there was some social security provision for the poor, who were no longer expected simply to fend for themselves. The New Deal meant that for the first time in the United States, central government directly affected how millions of its citizens were fed, housed, and educated. But it was not all good news. Some groups, such as farm workers, were not able to claim many benefits. This was also a time of severe drought. Thousands of poorer farmers were driven off the land and lost their homes and livelihoods. The rich were also hostile to the New Deal. Their taxes were increased, and many felt that too much government money was being spent on people who should look after themselves.

Roosevelt was one of America's most popular presidents, but despite the success of many of his projects, in 1939 over seven percent of Americans were still without jobs. Ironically it was World War II rather than the New Deal that brought about America's recovery from the Great Depression. The war boosted the U. S. economy, which grew faster than ever before or since. The experience in Europe, however, was very different.

Some of America's unemployed build roads for the government's work program.

World War II affected the lives of ordinary civilians in ways that no war before had done. Bombers flew into enemy territory and laid cities to waste. Over forty million people were uprooted from their homes. The destruction did not end with the return of peace. In the two years after the war, sixteen million Germans were expelled from the countries of central Europe. The long disruption of farming, trading, and factory life reduced the supply of basic necessities. In overcrowded cities, food was short. Rations in many parts of Germany were at starvation levels, with each person allowed only two slices of bread and margarine, a spoonful of porridge and two potatoes a day.

THE IRON CURTAIN

After the war ended in 1945, Germany was split among four of the victorious allies: Great Britain, the United States, France, and the Soviet Union. Communist eastern Europe (East Germany, Poland, Czechoslovakia, Hungary, Romania, Bulgaria, and Albania) was divided from western Europe by a frontier that came to be known as the "iron curtain."

Moving with all they can carry— civilians leave their devastated homes in Aachen, Germany, during World War II.

Bomb damage in Liverpool, England, during World War II

By 1948, a system of over 1,200 mi. (2,000 km) of barbed wire and sentry posts separated East from West. The Allies did not want to repeat the mistakes of the 1918 peace. Germany could never rebuild her shattered economy if people were so poverty-stricken that they did not have enough to eat. It was decided that the best way to prevent further upheaval, and stop the spread of Communism, was to give aid. In March 1948, the U.S. Congress voted to spend $4 billion on aid to Europe. Over the next four years, sixteen countries received a total of $13.5 billion under the Marshall Plan, as it was called. In return, they were expected to cooperate with each other and buy American goods.

KEY MOMENT

The Cold War

After the end of World War II, Europe became divided by politics and distrust. The United States and its allies feared the spread of Communism. The Soviet Union and countries under its control feared an American attack. This political stalemate became known as the Cold War. Although there was no direct fighting, an enormous amount of money was spent on weapons. The Cold War led to a global divide, as each side found different allies among southern nations and helped to fuel conflict there. Many countries diverted money into the costs of war and weapons rather than improving conditions for the poor. In 1991, after more than forty years, a combination of economic failure and declining Soviet influence led to the collapse of Communism in eastern Europe.

The welfare state—a mother in the UK collects her family allowance.

After World War II, freedom from poverty came to be seen by Western governments and people as a right that should be available to all. National leaders tried to make plans to share wealth more equally by taxing the better off and using the money to provide a variety of services for the poor. Some governments began to develop welfare states. One of the most radical of these was in Great Britain.

THE WELFARE STATE

Between 1945 and 1951, the Labour government in Great Britain made poverty relief a national goal. Even at the end of the 1930s, Great Britain was spending more money on social security than any other country in the world. Its citizens had, for the first time, a humane and extensive welfare system. The other countries of western Europe did not introduce welfare states as quickly as Britain. Most were too busy reorganizing their political systems. But although some spent more than others, they all set about meeting new standards in education, medical care, and housing.

The upheaval of war encouraged other world leaders into action against poverty. In 1944, politicians from forty-four countries met in New Hampshire. The Bretton Woods conference, as it was called, set up three new institutions. The World Bank would provide money for development projects, such as the building of roads, dams, and ports. The International Monetary Fund (IMF) would help countries remain financially stable. The General Agreement on Tariffs and Trade (GATT) would regulate world trade and prevent the sudden falls in commodity prices that had harmed so many countries.

Post-war American aid extended beyond Europe. These crates contain jeeps destined for Thailand.

Meanwhile, the "winds of change" were blowing across Africa and Asia. During the war, colonies had been called on to produce ever more cash crops for export as part of the war effort. But the thousands of troops who had fought had learned new lessons about human equality. One Nigerian soldier wrote: "...overseas soldiers are coming back home with new ideas. We have been told what we fought for. That is 'freedom.' We want nothing but freedom."

With the devastation of war, the former colonial powers were too weak to restore their old positions.

At the start of the Cold War, West Berlin was blockaded by the Soviet Union. The United States and Great Britain flew in all supplies. This airlift kept more than two million Germans from Communist rule.

In 1947, Great Britain granted independence to India. Over the coming decades, colonial rule was to end in most countries around the world.

World War II brought about immense changes. With the founding of welfare states, it seemed that at last a way had been found to "abolish want." But would this ideal be realized? And what was to become of poorer countries that could not afford welfare states? In the next chapter we will look in more detail at what different countries have done to alleviate poverty.

OPINION

"At the present moment in world history nearly every nation must choose between two alternative ways of life. The choice is too often not a free one.... I believe that we must assist free people to work out their own destinies in their own way. I believe that our help should be primarily through economic and financial aid... for the seeds of totalitarian regimes are nurtured by misery and want." From a speech by President Truman to Congress, March 12, 1947.

RESPONSES TO POVERTY

The post-war years were a time of prosperity and full employment in western Europe and the United States. Workers had more money to spend and industries were expanding to meet their demands. Electrical appliances, plastics, and car industries boomed.

In the United States, the state had already begun to play a greater role in the welfare of its citizens. Now the voices of the disadvantaged became louder. Black people, led by Martin Luther King, Jr. and others, formed the civil rights movement. They organized massive demonstrations to protest against their position as second-class citizens. The government could no longer ignore their demands.

President Lyndon Johnson holds up the "War on Poverty" bill, which he hoped would give all people a share in the country's prosperity.

In 1962, President John F. Kennedy spoke of crossing a "New Frontier" in the social and economic life of the country. He set a goal that continues to this day—to end poverty, rather than just to relieve it. Within two years Kennedy was dead, but his words had caught the imagination of the American public. His successor, Lyndon Johnson, declared a "War on Poverty" and pushed through laws that were associated with Kennedy's idealism. Welfare spending began to take off.

In western Europe, industries were now producing more than before the war. Living standards had begun to rise. In Great Britain, in 1950, Seebohm Rowntree published his third report on poverty. He claimed that child poverty had virtually died out. The welfare state, he said, was a prime reason for this. Government spending on welfare had grown enormously. In 1949, the first full year of welfare benefit, 13.5 percent of all monies spent by the government was spent on social security. By 1971, that figure had risen to 18 percent, and by 1997 it equaled 30 percent.

From July 1948 on, every person in Great Britain received free health care through the National Health Service.

THE CONSERVATIVE BACKLASH

In the 1980s, however, a new mood of conservatism took hold. Taxpayers resented rising welfare costs. When Ronald Reagan was elected president of the United States in 1980, he claimed that too many Americans were living on welfare rather than looking for work. Over the next three years, taxes were cut by between twenty-five and thirty percent. Programs to help the unemployed, single-parent families, and the low paid were slashed. The gap between rich and poor grew.

Not everyone benefited from rising prosperity in the industrial nations. This homeless man lies in front of the White House in Washington DC.

A similar policy was followed in Great Britain, where Margaret Thatcher was Conservative prime minister. These changes came at a time when the British economy was hit by the worst slump since the 1930s. In 1980, there was a sixty-four percent increase in the number of people out of work. The number of people living in poverty grew from five million in 1979 (nine percent of the population) to twelve million ten years later, or one person out of every five.

At the end of the twentieth century, state welfare systems seem to have reached their peak. They are now being reformed on both sides of the Atlantic. Societies are changing, and the reality of providing for everyone from the cradle to the grave is extremely expensive. Improved health care means that people now live longer. And with a population consisting of a higher proportion of older people, there are proportionally fewer younger people working to support those needing pensions and medical care.

WELFARE TO WORK

In 1996, President Bill Clinton promised to "end welfare as we know it." Those living on welfare now faced a requirement to work, and a five-year limit on benefits. At first welfare was denied to all immigrants, but this was later changed after protests. One year later, Clinton announced that more than a million people had found work and stopped receiving benefits. In Great Britain, there are plans to encourage the young and long-term unemployed to move from "welfare to work." There has also been a heated debate about whether lone parents should be expected to work.

It is still too early to predict the shape of welfare in years to come. Many fear that changes will result in greater hardship for the poor. They say that there are not enough jobs for everyone and that the state should continue to provide. Others argue that new

KEY MOMENT

The rediscovery of poverty

After Rowntree published his final report, there was a mood of optimism in Great Britain. With economic growth, poverty was finally disappearing. But in 1965 two social scientists, Abel-Smith and Townsend, published *The Poor and the Poorest*. They reported that, in 1960, nearly four million people were living in poverty. This publication was said to mark the "rediscovery of poverty." There was now a realization that social progress had failed to solve the poverty problem. Something had to be done urgently. At this time, important pressure groups were founded to campaign for welfare rights.

incentives will mean that those living on welfare will be encouraged to fend for themselves.

SURVIVING IN POOR COUNTRIES

Poorer countries cannot generally afford to provide social security for their people. Here the family offers an important safety net. Children in underdeveloped countries usually begin helping the family from a very young age, often by caring for younger brothers or sisters so that their mother can work. In rural areas they provide an extra pair of hands on the land. In cities they may be earning money by the time they are ten or eleven. When there are no pensions, children are a security for the future and take care of their parents in old age. This is not to say that the state has not also taken important steps to relieve poverty. Two countries that have taken very different paths are India and China. Both started with large sections of their population living in poverty and with similar resources.

In a country with no welfare system, these Somali children will care for their parents when they reach old age.

Women and children in India search a dump for scraps to recycle. The luxury apartment buildings of the rich rise up behind them.

KEY MOMENT

The Green Revolution
In the 1940s, scientists began to breed new kinds of food crops. These produced much more food but required high quantities of chemical fertilizer and pesticide. In the 1960s, India's "Green Revolution" took place, with the planting of these miracle seeds. Food production tripled between 1950 and 1987. But only the wealthier farmers could afford to grow the seeds. These farmers became richer. They bought the land of poorer farmers who could not afford to compete with them. As the poor farmers sold their land, they lost their livelihoods and sank further into poverty. Today, hunger is still a problem for the poor, and the gap between rich and poor has widened.

India achieved independence from Great Britain in 1947. The Indian prime minister, Jawaharlal Nehru, wanted his nation to benefit from the achievements of the industrialized countries. He saw development as a key to success. Today, India is one of the most important industrial countries in the world. It manufactures everything from electronic goods to cars and computer systems. But this has not benefited everyone. The unequal distribution of wealth in India means that about 320 million of its people still live in poverty. Although they live in the largest democracy in the world, they suffer poor health, lack basic education, and die at a younger age.

THE CHINESE REVOLUTION

In China, 1949 saw the Communist People's Liberation Army seize power. The Chinese revolution offered almost a fourth of the world's population a way out of the nightmare of grinding poverty, civil war, and famine. The Communists quickly redistributed the land more equally. By 1957, about ninety-seven percent of peasants had joined cooperatives where they shared land, machinery, and animals.

In 1958, Chairman Mao announced the "Great Leap Forward." This aimed to increase industrial and agricultural production dramatically. Peasants were moved into massive communes. However, as was the case with collective farms in the Soviet Union, food production rapidly declined. This combined with drought and flood to create the largest famine of the twentieth century. As many as twenty million people died.

Harvesting cotton in a commune in China. As many as 50,000 people would live and work in a commune.

Before the revolution, millions of Chinese people starved each year. Today, although there are twice as many people, most are adequately fed. Greater equality has made health and education services available to almost everyone. But these benefits have a price. Human rights in China are often ignored. Millions of people have died because they disagreed with Communist policies. An estimated ten million died during the years of the Cultural Revolution (1966–1976). And on June 4, 1989, many hundreds were killed and thousands injured when the government ended protests at Tiananmen Square, Beijing.

In China and India, resources need to be shared among many. Both countries have had to make difficult choices about the ways in which they provide for their people. In China, the state has made great efforts to try to divide wealth more fairly. One effect of this is that there is more state intervention in people's lives, and they often have less personal freedom. In India, the state has been less concerned with equality, but there are great gaps between rich and poor. However, Indians have more individual rights.

The Chinese government's concern with equality means that overall living standards are generally higher than in India. The average Chinese person lives twelve years longer than the average Indian. In India, hunger is a major problem; fifty percent of the children suffer from malnutrition. From the experiences of these two countries, which have had similar starting points, we can see that the steps governments take to end inequality can have a big effect on the fight against poverty.

All the countries we have looked at are trying to balance the well-being of their people with the resources they have available. This is much easier to achieve in the world's richer countries. But we should also remember that any state is made up of the people who live in it. All over the world, poor people are beginning to organize themselves to claim freedom from poverty. At the dawn of a new century, perhaps the best action any government can take is to listen to these voices.

These women in Bolivia have started a jam-making business— just one of many ways in which poor people are helping themselves.

THE CHANGING FACE OF AID

Aid can take many different forms. Here food is being brought into Liberia.

It is impossible to look at a history of poverty in the twentieth century without considering the help—or aid—that one country gives to another. There are many different types of aid. Besides sending money, food, and equipment, aid includes sending people abroad to teach their skills.

Most aid is given by governments. Organizations such as the United Nations and the World Bank are given money, which is then redistributed on behalf of the donor governments to countries that need it. Charities in the United States, Canada, and the UK, or NOVIB in the Netherlands, give far less aid than governments do. Although the amount they give is small—it amounts to less than ten percent of "official" aid—these organizations fill important gaps left by governments. They are committed to working with the poorest communities.

Often the impression is that all aid flows from rich to poor countries. In reality, it's a different picture. We have already seen how Marshall Aid helped to rebuild Europe after World War II. Today communities in Europe receive aid from the European Union. Southern Countries, such as India, also give aid to their neighbors.

KEY MOMENT

An aid target
In 1960, the United Nations agreed that rich countries should devote one percent of their Gross National Product (the total value of their goods and services) to aid poorer nations. This was later lowered to 0.7 percent, but only Norway, Denmark, Sweden, and the Netherlands have ever reached this target. In 1996, aid given by the rich countries amounted to 0.25 percent, the lowest level in twenty years.

Sometimes aid is used inappropriately. Money may be spent on weapons rather than people's well-being.

TIED AID

Although aid is often seen as a gift, the country that receives it (the recipient) is not usually free to decide how that money is spent. This is because aid is usually "tied." This means that the recipient has to buy goods or services from the donor country. Tied aid helps create jobs and develop industries in rich nations, but it can cause problems in the poor nations. Money may have to be spent on expensive equipment that is unsuitable for local conditions, or foreign experts may be brought in when local people can do the job just as well.

Social spending on education is of lasting benefit to the poor—these children are studying at a school in southern Pakistan.

In the first half of the twentieth century, there was no official aid from rich to poor countries: any relief for the poor was made by charities and missionaries. The years after World War II were a time of idealism. As former colonies achieved their independence, many felt that a Marshall Aid plan would help raise standards of living there too. But this idealism ignored an important problem. The economies of the colonies had been developed only for the profit of the colonial powers, who had extracted great wealth from the countries they dominated. The former colonies therefore had weak economies, with few of the basic building blocks for development in place. Levels of education, for example, were very low. In 1955, there was only one secondary school in the whole of French West and Equatorial Africa preparing Africans for higher education. With such disadvantages, it would be difficult for former colonies to work their way out of poverty.

DECADE OF DEVELOPMENT?

The United Nations declared the 1960s a "Decade of Development." It was widely believed that if poorer countries followed the same path as richer countries, poverty would eventually be ended. Industrialization was seen as a sign of progress. The World Bank, the

United Nations, and individual governments funded large-scale development projects such as dams and roads.

Ten years later it seemed that such economic growth had its costs for the poor. Dams, for example, had been seen as a great step forward. The electricity they provided lit up cities and powered factories. But poor people were forced off their land as it was flooded during construction. They lost their homes and livelihoods. Many of them moved to the cities and towns, where badly paid jobs provided them with little comfort.

In the 1970s, for the first time, aid was focused directly on the poor. In 1972, the president of the World Bank, Robert McNamara, suggested that aid should be aimed at meeting the basic needs of the poorest forty percent of the population. Social spending on food, welfare, health, and education was a top priority, because this would benefit the poorest most.

Children play near a dam on the Mekong River in China. Building dams often involves the forcible eviction of families from their land.

A free health clinic in Zimbabwe. Debt has forced the government to cut back on the services it provides to the poor.

The underdeveloped nations were also now making their voices heard. Aid, they said, was a poor substitute for a fairer deal. Their argument was vividly illustrated by the problems of debt.

THE DEBT CRISIS

In the 1970s, underdeveloped nations were encouraged to borrow money from the rich nations, particularly from large, commercial banks and the International Monetary Fund. They used this to pay for education and health services, and to industrialize. Some leaders also misused the money and spent it on projects that did not benefit the poor. In the mid-1980s, interest rates rose. Countries tried to export more raw materials to pay off their debts. But with so many countries competing to sell, prices fell. Between 1980 and 1993, the poorer nations lost around $100 billion as commodity prices plunged.

As a result, the 1980s were widely considered to be a lost decade for development. Governments were forced to cut back on health and education services in order to pay off their debts. In 1993, for every $1 given in aid, the rich nations took back $3 in debt repayments.

In the 1980s and 1990s, civil wars in countries such as Somalia, Bosnia, Rwanda, and Sudan changed the face of aid again. More and more aid was directed toward peacekeeping and emergencies. This aid is important for saving lives in the short term, but if lasting development is to take place, money and other resources need to be invested in health, education, and welfare services.

Casualties of Rwanda's civil war receive medical aid at a refugee camp.
Only lasting peace will end their poverty.

KEY MOMENT

The Brandt Commission

In 1980 an influential group of people met, with Willi Brandt, ex-chancellor of West Germany, as their chairman. They produced a report on the world's economic and social problems and likely future. The "Brandt Report" argued strongly for an increase in aid. The richer nations, it said, had a moral responsibility to help those less powerful than themselves. This was also in their own best interests, for the healthy future of the developed countries depended on the ending of poverty in the rest of the world.

GETTING AID TO THOSE WHO NEED IT

Over the past half century, much has been learned about how to make aid work better. It may seem obvious that it is very important to make sure that it reaches those who need it most. But the United Nations has reported that the poorest forty percent of people in the poor nations receive much less aid per head than the richest forty percent. This is partly because countries use aid for political reasons. During the Cold War, West Germany refused to give aid to any country that recognized East Germany. And European Union aid to Egypt rose by over 400 percent because this country was Europe's ally during the Gulf War in 1991.

It is vital that aid reaches the people who need it most, such as these children at a refugee camp in southeast Turkey.

The quality of aid is as important as the quantity. It is important that aid be used to help countries and communities in the long term. Spending money on education, for example, means that in the future the poor will have a better chance of earning a living. If less aid were tied, countries would be free to buy what they needed, rather than what donors wanted to sell them. Giving poor people a say in their own future aid programs would be more likely to succeed. And thinking in the longer term about how aid projects might affect whole communities or the environment will protect the needs of future generations.

In donor countries too, ordinary people have strong opinions about aid. Over the last twenty-five years, public concern about poverty has grown. Most people believe that aid is a good thing. A survey in the European Union found that seventy percent of people felt that their government should increase its aid budget.

AID AND THE MEDIA

One reason for the growing public awareness about aid is media reporting. In the rich nations, news coverage of disasters brings images of people undergoing traumatic events into every household. These images

> **KEY MOMENT**
>
> **The Ethiopian famine**
> On October 23, 1984, BBC News carried an item on famine in the northern Ethiopian province of Wollo. This seven-minute report was subsequently shown by 425 television stations all over the world, illustrating how powerful the role of the media is in international human affairs. The numbers of those who died in the famine between 1983 and 1985 are thought to be between 500,000 and one million. The reaction to the famine was unprecedented. The musician, Bob Geldof, caught the imagination of a new generation of young people with a series of tours and rock concerts entitled Live Aid, which raised millions in one year.

The series of Live Aid concerts around the world fired up a generation of young people and focused public attention on famine in Africa.

prompt outpourings of generosity; but there are drawbacks too. Poor people are often seen as passive victims in these simplified pictures. Little attention is paid to the ways in which they are helping themselves. Ignoring the strengths and abilities of the poor can lead those who give to feel that their efforts are of no value, because the problems do not seem to end.

Perhaps this helps to explain why the amount of aid that governments give is falling. In 1996, as richer nations concentrated on internal concerns, amounts of official aid reached their lowest level since statistics began in 1950. This might not be such a problem if the poor nations were not faced with massive debts and a world trade system that keeps commodity prices low. But while the gaps between rich and poor countries remain, aid will continue to play a vital role in improving people's lives.

Aid for the poorest—a small loan for livestock means that this woman in Bangladesh is now able to support her family.

LOOKING TO THE FUTURE

Throughout the twentieth century, great advances have been made in the war on poverty. The early years of the century saw the beginnings of state welfare systems in Great Britain, Denmark and Germany. In the years following World War II, poverty was reduced in eastern Europe and the Soviet Union. And, as colonies became independent, they made enormous efforts to improve the standards of living of their people. Some of the world's poorest countries, such as China, have made the greatest advances. In the last twenty years China has halved the proportion of its people living below the poverty line. According to the United Nations, world poverty has fallen more in the past fifty years than in the previous five hundred.

However, this progress has not been without set-backs. At the end of a century that has offered possibilities unimaginable a hundred years ago, it is a cruel truth that one person in every four lives on less than one dollar a day. Crueller still is the fact that the gap between the rich and the poor is growing. In 1960, the richest one-fifth of the world's people had thirty times more wealth than the poorest fifth. By 1991, they had sixty-one times more.

Young people are especially vulnerable to poverty. Even in wealthy nations, young homeless people are becoming an increasingly common sight.

POVERTY IN THE NORTH

Richer countries are usually in a stronger position than poorer ones to meet the needs of their citizens. But, as we have seen, this does not mean that poverty is confined to the poor countries of the world. In the United States, which has the world's largest industrial economy, there are at least 324,000 people without homes and at least 500,000 underfed children. Nearby Cuba is one of the poorest countries in Latin America. Yet it has one of the best health care systems in the world and the rate of death among young children is lower than that in Washington, D.C. Poverty persists in other rich countries too. According to the UK Child Poverty Action Group, one in three children in Great Britain lives below the poverty line; ten million people cannot afford adequate housing; 4.6 million working people are living in poverty; and 35,000 people die prematurely every year because they cannot afford to keep warm.

People learning about the importance of clean water. Simple measures can dramatically improve the quality of people's lives.

Such observations can lead to claims that poverty will always be with us. Yet the costs of ending deprivation are less than people imagine. Providing basic social services such as health care and education to all the world's people would cost about $80 billion. This is less than 0.5 percent of the world's income and less than the wealth of the world's seven richest men.

Many people argue that population growth is a major cause of poverty. While it is certainly true that the number of people on our planet is growing fast, the picture may not be as gloomy as it has been painted. At the beginning of this century, families in the world's richer countries were much larger than they are today. Gradually improvements in health care came about, with the introduction of antibiotics and vaccinations. As families enjoyed higher living standards, fewer people died young. This led to a rapid population growth. Now, however, because people in the developed countries expect to live longer, they have fewer children.

Some countries have taken radical steps to control their populations. This poster advertises the Chinese government's policy on limiting families to just one child.

In poor nations, families tend to be larger because death rates are still high. When there is a risk that children may fall sick and die, people tend to have more children to improve the chance that some of them will live to adulthood. Most population experts now agree that population growth is a result rather than a cause of poverty. When the high death rates caused by poverty fall, then so will population figures.

In 1950 there were two billion people in the world. Today this figure has more than doubled. It is predicted that by the middle of the twenty-first century there will be ten billion people in our world. Perhaps one of the greatest problems for the future is not over-population, but how we use what our planet provides. A child born in a rich country consumes far more than a child born in a poor country. The rich nations currently use up eighty percent of the world's resources. Our world is capable of sustaining all its people, but only if we learn to share what we have.

OPINION

"We must recognize that we are living in a time-bomb and unless we take action now, it could explode in our children's faces."
James Wolfensohn, president of the World Bank, talking in 1996 about easing the debt problems of the world's poorest countries so that the burden of poverty can be lifted from them

POVERTY

KEY MOMENT

The poor protest
About eight million children in Brazil spend their days on the streets trying to earn a living, but deprived of opportunities such as getting an education. Living in poverty, they have often been the victims of violent attacks and even murder. In 1989, they came together and marched on the Brazilian parliament. Their action resulted in a change in the law that now offers them some protection against violence.

Street children in Brazil with a "legal."
This is a type of currency that can be
exchanged. As it is not real money,
children are less likely to be robbed.

OUR SHARED WORLD

Changes in communications, trade patterns, technology, and travel all help us realize that our world is a shrinking place. What happens in distant places changes our lives too. Whether we are rich or poor, poverty affects us all. In the face of growing hardship, countries are being forced to use up their natural resources in the most profitable way possible.

Our global environment suffers as precious forests are cut down. Across the world, trees are disappearing ten times faster than they are being planted and global warming is a growing threat to us all. Deprivation also creates social unrest and war. Between 1945 and 1995, nearly twenty-two million people have died in wars. Millions more have been injured or become refugees. Poverty divides societies and keeps whole generations from using their skills and talents to build a better future.

58

As we look toward the next century, we may be excited about the positive progress that can be made and worried about the poverty that remains. Millions of people feel the same way. We are all citizens of a shared world. As the twenty-first century dawns, we need to face the challenge of ending poverty together.

As pressure on land increases, poor people are forced to open up new areas for cultivation and trees are cut down in the process. These Sri Lankan children are planting trees in a deforested area.

GLOSSARY

Absolute poverty a condition in which a person is deemed not to have enough to meet basic survival needs, e.g. sufficient food, water, or shelter.

Aid money grants and other help given by one country to another. "Official" aid is given by governments and agencies such as the UN. "Unofficial" aid is given by charities.

Cash crops crops that are grown for export rather than for local use.

Collectivization the process by which farmland in Communist countries is taken over by the state.

Colonialism the policy and practice of a country or people in extending control over other peoples or areas. Historically, colonies had no real independence and were used by the colonial powers to gain access to raw materials and markets for exports.

Commodity a cash crop or raw material that is traded.

Commune a group of collective farms in which all land and many other articles are owned equally by all the inhabitants. Communes in China are also units of local government and provide education and welfare.

Communism a political system that calls for the elimination of private property and the distribution of wealth according to need.

Conservatism opposition to rapid change. Conservatism is a system of beliefs that seeks to promote individual effort and private ownership.

Discrimination the act of treating people unfairly because of their race, language, religion, culture, or political beliefs.

GNP (Gross National Product) the total value of goods and services in a country. GNP is commonly used to measure a country's wealth.

Hierarchy a system in which people are organized by rank, with those above giving orders to those below.

Human rights rights that every human being is entitled to.

Hyperinflation an economic situation in which money loses value very quickly.

Indigenous peoples people who have lived in a place (and close to the land) from the earliest times.

Industrial Revolution the change from an agricultural to an industrial economy. The Industrial Revolution took place in Europe (and subsequently the United States) during the eighteenth and nineteenth centuries. This time saw the rapid growth of cities.

Interest a charge made when money is loaned. When people or countries lend money they expect to get back more than they lend. This extra is called interest.

Panhandler A person who asks passersby for money.

Philanthropy practical help given to the poor, often by rich individuals. Philanthropy was an important part of poor relief before the state played a more active role in giving assistance.

Pressure groups organizations set up to press for social change. In the 1970s many pressure groups were set up to campaign for welfare rights.

Raw materials materials used in manufacturing, e.g. wood, oil, and minerals such as coal or gold.

Refugees People forced to leave their country because of violence or persecution.

Relative poverty a condition in which a person is deemed not to have enough to lead a full life compared with other people in the community.

Reparations money demanded by the victors in a war to compensate for damage done.

Social security money collected in taxes and paid out by the state to provide assistance to those who need it, such as the unemployed, the sick, and the elderly.

Stock market a financial center where shares are traded. Ownership of shares in a company gives a person the right to a share of that company's profits.

Subsistence farming a type of farming in which almost everything that is produced by a family or community is consumed by them, rather than sold for cash.

Tied aid aid that is given "with strings attached." Donor countries may demand that money be spent on certain products.

Welfare state a system in which the government collects money in taxes to provide social security for the less well-off.

BOOKS TO READ

For younger readers:

Fyson, Nance. *The Development Puzzle: A Sourcebook for Learning About the Rich/Poor Divide, an Effort Towards One World Development.* New York: Oxford University Press, 1991.
A detailed account of aspects of development and interdependence.

Garlake, Teresa. *The Rich-Poor Divide* (Global Issues series). Austin, TX: Thomson Learning, 1996.
Describes the growing division between the richest and the poorest people in the world. Features stories from many countries.

Hubbard, Jim. *Lives Turned Upside Down: Homeless Children in their Own Words and Photographs.* New York: Simon & Schuster, 1996.

Roleff, Tamara L. (editor) *The Homeless: Opposing Viewpoints.* San Diego, CA: Greenhaven, Press, 1995.

Winters, Paul A. (editor). *Welfare: Opposing Viewpoints.* San Diego, CA: Greenhaven Press, 1997.

Witness History series, various authors and dates, Wayland
Analysis of key issues within a subject, including a wide selection of source material. Titles include *Britain Between the Wars, Britain Since 1945, China Since 1945, The Cold War, The Rise of Fascism, The Russian Revolution, The Third Reich, The USA Since 1945,* and *The USSR Under Stalin.*

Wolf, Bernard. *Homeless.* New York: Orchard Books, 1995.

Background and reference books for adults:

A - Z of World Development by Wayne Ellwood (editor), New Internationalist Publications, 1998
An important and accessible reference book on key themes, containing over 600 entries.

Atlas of World Development by Tim Unwin (editor). New York: John Wiley and Sons Ltd, 1995
A reference book containing useful maps to highlight development issues.

The Development Dictionary by Wolfgang Sachs (editor). Zed Press, 1992
A collection of essays on themes such as equality, resources and the role of the state, which questions the whole basis for twentieth century development.

Human Development Report, published annually for the United Nations Development Program (UNDP). New York: Oxford University Press
An annual report that contains a different key message each year. The report includes essential statistical information highlighting human development issues.

The Oxfam Poverty Report by Kevin Watkins, Oxfam, 1995
Analysis of the state of world poverty, setting out an agenda for change.

Poor Citizens: the State and the Poor in Twentieth Century Britain by David Vincent, Longman, 1996
A powerful and moving book that surveys the role of the state in alleviating poverty in twentieth-century Britain.

Poverty: the Facts by Carey Oppenheim, Child Poverty Action Group, 1996
A comprehensive booklet on poverty in Britain and Europe, looking at the causes and current debates.

Poverty and Development in the 1990s by Tim Allen and Alan Thomas (editors). New York: Oxford University Press, 1992.
A detailed introduction to some of the major issues of world poverty, with twenty themed chapters written by specialist authors.

USEFUL ADDRESSES

The following organizations are likely to provide either further information or educational material for young people and their teachers.

UNITED STATES

InterAction
1717 Massachusetts Avenue NW, Suite 801,
Washington, DC 20036

United Nations Development Program
1 UN Plaza
New York, NY 10017

UK

Child Poverty Action Group
1-5 Bath Street
London, UK EC1V 9PY

Oxfam
274 Banbury Road
Oxford, UK OX2 7DZ

Save the Children
Mary Datchelor House, 17 Grove Lane
London, UK SE5 8RD.

World Development Movement
25 Beehive Place
London, UK SW9 7QR

AUSTRALIA

Australian Council for Overseas Aid
Private Bag 3
Deakin ACT, Australia 2600

Community Aid Abroad
156 George Street
Fitzroy, Vic, Australia 3065

INDEX

Numbers in **bold** refer to
illustrations.

aborigines **21**
absolute poverty 6
aid **35**, 46–54, **46**
Ambedkar, Dr. B. R. 19

Berlin Airlift **36–37**
Berlin Conference 13
Beveridge, William 34
Brandt Commission 9, 51
Bretton Woods Conference 35
Buddhism **7**, 19

cash crops 12, 28, 36
caste system 18–19
charities 6, **7**, 25, 30, 48
Child Poverty Action Group 56
civil rights movement 38
civil war 51, **51**
Clinton, Bill 41
Cold War 33, **36–37**, 52
collectivization 29, **29**, 44
colonies 8, 12–13, 18, 27, 36–37,
    48, 55
Columbus, Christopher 9
communes **44**
Communism 21, 33, 44
Communist People's Liberation
    Army 44
cooperatives 44
Cultural Revolution 44

Debs, Eugene V. 16
debt 50–51, 54, 57
"deserving" poor 6
development projects 49, **49**
donor countries 46–47, 52, 53
drought 29, 31, 44

European Union 46, 52, 53
extended family 42, **42**

factory workers 11, **11**,
famine
    in China 44
    in Ethiopia 53
    in Russia **28**, 29

Gandhi, Mohandas 19, **19**
Geldof, Bob 53
General Agreement on Tariffs and
    Trade (GATT) 35
Great Depression 24–29, 30, 31
Great Leap Forward 44
Green Revolution 43
Gulf War 52

"harijans" *see* "untouchables"
Hitler, Adolf 17, 26
homelessness 5, **40, 55**
human poverty index 7
human rights 44
Hunger Campaign 45
Hunger Marches 25
hyperinflation 26, **27**

immigration 17, **17**, 41
indigenous peoples 21, **21**
Industrial Revolution 11, 15
International Monetary Fund 35,
    50
"iron curtain" 32–33

Johnson, Lyndon **38**, 39

Kennedy, John F. 39
King, Martin Luther, Jr. 38

Lenin, Vladimir Ilyich 20–21, **20**,
    29
Live Aid 53, **53**
loans, small **54**
London, Jack 5

Maasai **14**
malnutrition 45
Mandela, Nelson 18
Marshall Aid 46, 48
Marshall Plan 33
middle classes 16
migrant labor 13, 20, 49
missionaries 13, **13**, 48
Mohammed 6

National Health Service **39**
National Socialism 26–27
Nehru, Jawaharlal 43
Nixon, Richard 46
NOVIB 46
Nyerere, Julius 54

Orwell, George 15

peasants 20–21, 29, **29**, 44
philanthropists 4, 11
plague 55
Poor and the Poorest, The 41
poor nations 8, 33, 36, 42, 46–47,
    50, 51, 52, 54, 57
population growth 56–57, **57**

Reagan, Ronald 40
refugees 5, 7, **51, 52**, 58
relative poverty 7
reparations bill 26
rich nations 8, 47, 50, 51, 53, 56,
    57
rich-poor divide 8–9, **8–9**, 13, 18,
    55
Rockefeller, John D. 11, 17
Roosevelt, Franklin D. 30–31
    and New Deal 30
Rowntree, Seebohm 4, 11, 39, 41
Russian Revolution 20–21, **20**, 29
Rwanda 51, **51**

slave trade 9–11, **10**,

slums 11

social spending 48–52, 56

soup kitchens 25

South Africa 12, 18, **18**
    apartheid in 18
    1913 Land Act 18

Stalin, Josef 29

starvation 32, 44

street children **5**, 58, **58**

subsistence societies 9, 14, **14**

Tawney, R. H. 9

Thatcher, Margaret 41

Tiananmen Square 44

Treaty of Versailles 17

"undeserving" poor 6

unemployment 25, **25**, 26, 28, 29,
    30, **30–31**, 40–41

United Nations 46, 47, 48–49, 52,
    55

United Nations Development
    Program 7

"untouchables" 18–19, **19**

upper classes 15, **15**

Wall Street Crash **23**, 24, **24**, 25,
    27

"War on Poverty" bill **38**, 39

welfare spending 34, 39–42

welfare state 34, **34**, 37, 39, 55

"welfare to work" 41

women and poverty 21, **43**, **45**,
    54

working classes 16–17, **16**

World Bank 35, 46, 49, 57

Works Progress Administration
    (WPA) 30–31, **30–31**

World War I 17, 20, 22, **22**

World War II 29, 31, 32–33, **32**,
    33, 34, 36–37, 46, 48, 55